A Short History Of Cork

by

W. G. Mac Carthy

Killeen

First published in this format
in 1996 by
Killeen Books,
Killeen,
Blackrock Village,
Cork City.

The text of this short history comprises W.G. Mac
Carthy's History of Cork (which was first published
in 1869 by Francis Guy of Cork and originally
presented as a lecture to the Cork Scientific and
Literary Society) and additional material by Pat
Cotter.

ISBN 1-873548-32-X

This book is printed in Dublin by Colour Books on
acid free Munken paper. Acid free paper will not
discolour or grow brittle with age.

I.—THE CELTIC PERIOD.
(From 580 to 846)

The earliest glimpse history has given us of Cork is towards the end of the sixth century; and the central figure this glimpse reveals is that of the founder of the city, Lochan the Fair-haired, since called St. Finnbarr. He was born near Galway. He studied under a Roman ecclesiastic. He became a scholar, a monk, and a priest. He lived for some years at Gougane, called Barra after him. Thence he came hither. Here he founded a monastery and opened a school. Before he died the monastery had become a famous abbey; the school had grown into an university; and around abbey and university had grown up the city of Cork. Thus was our city founded.

The abbey, the university, the city, throve for two hundred and fifty years. Let us look back through the ages and try to form some idea of them.

What was the Abbey like? It was situated in the suburb we still call Gill Abbey, near where now stands the Queen's College. It spread southward to the little lake we call "the Lough". It included the present Protestant cathedral, still called after St. Finnbarr. According to Petrie, its church, library, refectory, and other principal buildings, were of stone, surrounded by a wall pierced with square-headed doorways, and crowned by the round tower (whose foundations were only recently removed,) which served the triple purpose of a keep for sacred vessels and precious books, a watch-tower against enemies, and a belfry to call to prayer. The Abbey lands spread round about. The monks and students lived in little wooden, skin-roofed houses. Of material comfort there was probably little; of material splendour there was certainly none. Yet I think every Cork man may be proud of the old Abbey of Cork. It did work in its day: it made Cork more famous than ever Cork was since.

What were the monks at? They certainly were not sluggards. For one thing they were farming. Our agriculture is still backward: how defective it must have been then! How useful to introduce agricultural arts of Gaul and Italy to this far-off spot in the Western Seas! Literary culture and teaching ranked next among their avocations. It was a speciality of Irish monks that they were ardent scholars and earnest teachers. Their teaching being sought in every capital of Europe, is proof that they learned and taught well. Their chief duties, however, were religious and missionary. Christianity had been only recently introduced into Ireland. Vast tracts and tribes were still pagan, or nearly so. The Abbey of Cork was a sort of outpost in the work of Christianisation. Dungarvan owes its name, and Waterford its Christianity, to Brother Garvan, of the Abbey of Cork. Brother Coleman became the missionary bishop and patron saint of Cloyne; Brother Fachnan, of Ross; Brother Nessan, of Mungret; another Coleman, of Ossory; Brother Brian, of St. Brienne in France; and in the north of Scotland brave sons of St. Finnbarr gave his patronage to the city of Caithness, and his name to the Island of Barra.

What was the University like? Materially, it was a poor concern; intellectually, not so. It was one of those great Irish schools which were the glory of the time. I think it is as well proved as anything in history that these schools *were* glorious. Shrewd Sam Johnson thought so; and he had no prejudices in favour of Ireland. So did Belarmine and Muratori; Mabillon and Denina; Mosheim, Scaliger, and Niebuhr; Schlegel, Görres and Döllinger; Cousin, Thierry, and Michelet; Hallam, Newman, and Macaulay. It seems safe to conclude that they were not all mistaken. Civilisation had, to use Görres happy phrase, taken up its "winter quarters" in Ireland. Wintry times it certainly had of it throughout Europe. The Roman Empire of the West had fallen. The various tribes of the North had settled down amidst its ruins: the Angles and Saxons in Britain; the Franks in Gaul; the Goths in Germany; the Vandals and Lombards in Italy; the Huns in Rome itself. Of course the old inhabitants were terrified, and had cause to be so. Equally, of course, the conquerors scarce knew what to do with themselves. But Ireland remained uninvaded. As she had escaped the eagles of the South, so she had hitherto escaped the ravens of the North. And just then her keen Celtic intellect had seized, together with the truths of Christianity, all the secular learning of the time. Her abbeys had recently been founded; her schools opened. Hither fled the timid for safety and the learned for leisure, bringing with them their best books and finest tastes. Hither also came the aspiring and the inquisitive. The Romance citizen sent his sons to the schools of Erin for the culture which had become almost impossible at home; and the sons of the conquerors sought from the gentle and scholarly Celt the instruction they would have disdained from the men whom their race had subdued. The occasion was a great one; and our fathers were equal to it. They received students from all lands; they went to all lands to teach. To them Alfred came to learn; from them Charlemagne received professors. Ireland became, as Johnson said, "the School of the West". Scaliger writes that at this period "nearly all the learned were from Ireland". The Universities of Oxford, Paris, and Pavia were of Irish origin. There is scarcely an important continental city from Palermo to Cologne in which some Irish saint and scholar is not still reverenced. It was of this great movement that the university of Cork took part; and it was thus that in the old days, by banks of our old river, the olive-tinted son of the South met the blue-eyed Saxon; Hun read with Gaul; Angle with Iberian; and all with O'Mahonys from Drohid-Mahon, O'Driscoll's of Inberscheine, O'Sullivans Beare, and O'Sullivans Bantriagh, and O'Sullivans of Dunkerron, MacGillicuddys and O'Donoghues of the far West, and MacCarthys, to whom every tribe owed allegiance, from the Shannon to the sea.

But the city of Cork: what was it like in the Celtic time? It was situated on the low-lying island where now run the North and South Main Streets. The Marsh ("Corcach"),on which it stood, gave it its name. It must have been a place of some importance, as it is called by the annalists "Great Cork"; and the MacCarthys gave up their older titles for that of Kings of Cork. It was built of wood. Some of the houses, probably, were of good construction, like those wooden houses which still linger in Continental cities. I fear most of them were mere sheelings, or mud huts. Still a city in constant intercourse with the best European life of the time must have been far from uncivilised. It had some commerce, too. The ships that brought students carried merchandise; and we read of Cork merchants in traffic with Merovingian kings. Metallurgy was practised, and linen stuff made. It was governed by a well-defined code of laws, still to be read. If it had not, as Cork has now, seventy attorneys, it had several brehons. Its ollambs practised both in physic and in literature. Instead of four daily newspapers, it had I don't know how many *dresbdearteachs*, or public storytellers. It had commenced that work of reclamation of the marshes, which, after a thousand years, is still unfinished. Its sons helped the monks to teach and the MacCarthys to fight. No doubt, its daughters taught some of the foreign students—to love. So praying, learning, teaching, trading, fighting, loving, Abbey and University and City went on for more than two hundred and fifty years.

II.—THE DANISH PERIOD.
(From 846 to 1172)

In the early part of the ninth century Cork shared the consternation that was caused throughout Europe by the terrible sea-rovers of Denmark. Even then they harassed every coast from Norway to Sicily. They penetrated Ireland, England, France. Charlemagne wept when he saw their black banners in the Mediterranean. Soon after they conquered England, and seized the fairest provinces of France. It would, of course, be unsafe to take their character from their foes; but not even the faltering records and vehement denunciations of annalists, whose hands trembled as they wrote, give so vivid an idea of their ferocity as their own chronicles. Those reveal a spirit almost demoniac. The blood mounts to one's temples as one reads. Murder, rapine, plunder, ruthless cruelty, are the substance of them, made all the more fearful by a faint glimmer of poetic beauty that plays over them, like a moonbeam on a black and seething sea. The worship of Odin was the most baleful of superstitions. He was adored under the titles of " The Incendiary," "The Bloodthirsty," "The Unsparing". Homicide was deemed a virtue, pity a weakness; death glorious only when found in battle. Hear a scald in praise of his hero:—

" Know ye not TORQUETIL ? Fear ye not the torch of his face?
His dreadful presence makes the crash of arms more fatal;
His hand was never yet withheld from bloodshed;
His heart is ignorant of the feeling of forgiveness.
The groans of the dying, the shrieks of the despairing mother,
The wail of the young infant, turn him not aside.
Wherever he treads, the very earth is robbed of her fleece
And the naked coasts he leaves after him confess his power."

Such were the ideals of heroism that the sea-bards sung and the sea-kings imitated. They sailed forth every spring from the fjords of Norseland, to seek plunder or a home on the shores and islands of Europe. Reared for war alone, in war they were terrible. A seafaring people for a thousand years, their ships were superior to any of the time. Hardy and adventurous, boasting that they never slept under a roof or drained a bowl on a sheltered hearth, it is not wonderful that even the sturdy Saxon and the chivalrous Frank fled before their faces. Sad was the day when their gilded prows touched any shore. "They marched," say the *Four Masters*, "escorted by fire." "As they passed," says Henry of Huntingdon, "they gaily partook of the repast unwillingly offered, and paid for their cheer by burning the house and killing the host." They loved the blood of priests and the gold of churches. They lodged their horses in the chapels of kings. "And when they had wasted a Christian country," says Thierry, "they would say in derision, 'We have sung the mass of the lances: it began at the rising of the sun.' "

Such were the Danes when they conquered Cork. They first came in 820. They plundered the Abbey, ruined the University, and burned the City. They came again in eighteen years and repeated the process. In 846 they took possession of the lower part of the city, and settled in it. I find the Four Masters speak of Cork as a "Danish fort" that very year. But here, as elsewhere in Ireland, they seem to have been resisted with singular tenacity, stubbornness, and success. The southern hill, with the Abbey, was held against them from first to last. They often plundered it; and this is what is meant when we read in the *Four Masters* that Cork was "plundered by the Danes" at the very time that we are told "the Danes were in possession of Cork". It was the Irish city on the hill they plundered. The MacCarthys often "returned the compliment" to the fort in the valley. It must have been a dreary time. Gallant feats of arms, no doubt, were done, and, I hope, many a gentle deed of mercy. But there was no more peace by fair Lough Eire: the poor monks must have been half soldiers by this time. No more students from foreign lands: they dared not come to this poor little beleaguered, dismembered fragment of a city. Thus, foot to foot in mortal feud, they stood for two full centuries.

At length the raven standard was trampled down, and the terrible strangers yielded. Their lives were spared. The rovers became citizens. They paid allegiance and tribute to the MacCarthy, who was once more acknowledged King of Cork. A portion of the city and adjoining country were set apart for them. This district was for centuries subsequently known as "the Ostmen's Cantred". Soon after they became Chieftains. They applied themselves to trade. Their maritime and ship-building skill proved of good service. They may be said to have founded the character of Cork as a commercial community. Their ferocity gave way to the influences of religion and civilisation. Their vigour, courage, and self-reliance remained. They became good subjects of the MacCarthys, and good neighbours of the Abbey. Scandinavian sages sing, of match-makings between Norse kings and Milesian princesses. The descendants of the Danish invaders are amongst our best and oldest Cork families—Goulds, Gallways, Coppingers, Terrys, Skiddys—and it is neither unsafe nor uncomplimentary to say that there are few Cork men who have not in their veins some tincture of the blood of the adventurous North. But though the city revived, the University and Abbey never recovered. Curiously enough, it is from the famous Abbot of Clairvaux, the great St. Bernard himself, we get particulars of an effort made to restore them. This effort was made by his friend St. Malachy, with the co-operation of Dermot Mac Carthy, king of Munster, and Gill Adha O'Mughin, Bishop of Cork. The bishop introduced a new discipline. The King gave a new charter (still extant,) and a princely endowment. Everything promised success. But in the midst of his labours the Bishop died. And in that same year the Normans came.

III.—THE NORMAN PERIOD.
(From 1172 to 1603)

In 1172 Ireland was invaded by the daring and brilliant race who had previously settled in Normandy and conquered England. The surrender of Cork to them by King Dermot MacCarthy was the first great success of the invasion. Why Dermot did it no one can tell; perhaps it was because the old king had married a young Norman wife. That he soon regretted the surrender of his capital is certain. Before the year was out he was thundering at its gates. They opened to their prince. The Norman garrison was turned out. The towns people rallied. The sons of the sea-rovers fitted out thirty ships, and sailed for Waterford, where lay the Norman host. King Mac Carthy followed by land, But both were defeated. The Norman was no contemptible foe. He was accustomed to conquer. His mailed armour was almost impervious to the light arrows of the Irish archers. His great Flemish horses rode down the Kerry ponies. His heavy battle-axes and slashing broadswords clove through the wicker shields of the kernel. At sea his advantage was still greater; for in the ports of Normandy and England the shipbuilding arts of the North had been improved by all that was known of Phoenician, Greek, and Roman skill, and a beginning was made of that maritime supremacy which England has so long enjoyed.

I do not find it recorded how the Normans regained Possession of Cork. That they did so almost immediately is certain. The very successor of Gill Adha was a Norman prelate. They never afterwards lost it. The MacCarthys gave them "a hot life of it;" shut them up in it like prisoners; besieged them again and again; and scarcely left them a year's rest for centuries. But they were reinforced from England and France. Brilliant Norman knights, with their haughty airs and splendid accoutrements, their noble ladies, their troubadours and esquires their archers and their cavalry; sturdy Saxon artisans, seeking, in a new country the peace they had lost at home; Aquitanian merchants seeking trade, and Gascon rovers seeking adventure —a motley crowd, speaking, various tongues, of various manners and traditions—poured into the little Irish city, and made common cause against the native race. Their blood is in all our veins; their names run through all our succeeding annals—Barrys, Roches, Powers, Fitzgeralds, and so on. The Celtic inhabitants either fled into the country, or yielded to their conquerors, or gathered under the shadow of St. Finnbarr's on the hill. The southern suburb became known as "the Irish" or "old town". As in the time of the Danes, it was often held as a redoubt against "the strangers"—so, for many a century, the Normans were called. These latter made the Danish town upon the island their home. They fortified it, in the Norman manner, with massive walk, serried towers, and castellated forts, the remains of which were, until recently, to be seen. The double-branching river formed a foss. North and south, beneath a high, portcullis, was a drawbridge. The space inside the walk was very narrow—one long street, with the breadth of an arrow's cast on either side. Cork was, indeed, rather a fortress than a city. Within this restricted enclosure the houses were built in narrow streets and lanes, whose high pitched Norman gables, and projecting windows still linger in our older localities. Churches were built, and even abbeys. Castles within the very fortress itself, such as Skiddy's and Roche's Castles, testified to internal strife. As time advanced, the population overflowed these narrow limits, and a timid suburb crept up either hill. The Barrys were bolder, and their Castle of Shandon soon stood out from the north. The Gallways' old fort at the south corresponded to it at the other side. But the Norman monks were still bolder than the Norman barons. They had reason. They knew that in the fiercest fray the Irish respected the altar of their common God. The Augustinian Eremites soon had a convent and a church outside the walk towards the south—the "Red Abbey", whose tower still stands in Cumberland-street. The "Black Friars," or Dominicans had a house in the same direction—"Santa Maria de Insula " (St. Mary's of the Isle). John, Earl of Morton before the twelfth century closed founded the Abbey of St. John, also outside the walls. Nor did the native races fail to reciprocate this generosity. Within a stone's cast of North Gate, Mac Carthy More built and endowed the "North Abbey" for the "Grey Friars", as the Franciscans were called. His tomb stood in the midst of the choir. The house, from its discipline, was called "The Mirror of Ireland". Under its solemn aisles and in its sepulchral vaults, men of all races forgot their differences, and were united in life and in death.

Together with their fighting and their praying, Cork folk, at this period, seem to have found time to do some practical joking. One joke of theirs "took in" the King of France and threatened to dethrone the King of England. It was about Perkin Warbeck. Warbeck was a handsome young Fleming, who chanced to visit Cork in 1492 with his master, a Breton merchant. "Arrayed" (as the poor fellow tells us in his dying declaration) " with some clothes of silk" belonging, to "his said master", he looked very fine. Some Cork wag, suggested that he was the son of the Duke of Clarence, who had lately been in Dublin. Warbeck denied it. The jokers brought him before the mayor. Warbeck declared on oath that he was not the duke's son, or of his blood. But the jokers were not satisfied. One of them, John Walters (who became Mayor of Cork the following year), proposed to him to give out that he was the Duke of York, whom men believed to have been murdered by Richard III in the Tower. The vain young Fleming assented. He learned English, and was supplied by his Cork friends with splendid attire and retinue. As soon as he was trained to act his part, Walters, then mayor, boldly wrote to the Lord-Deputy and the King of France to announce the existence and the rights of the newly-discovered heir of England. The Deputy seems to have been cautious, and found an excuse for not answering; but the King was "taken in". He invited Warbeck to the court of France. Thither, nothing daunted, Warbeck went. He was received with royal honours. He had even the audacity to palm himself on the Duchess of Burgundy as her nephew. She, too, was "taken in". She supplied him with men and money. He landed in Kent, and raised his banner as Richard IV, King of England. Meeting some disasters, he returned to his old patrons at Cork. Here he was joined by the Earl of Desmond. Walters and his friends also joined him. After an attempt on Waterford they sailed for Cornwall, and laid siege to Exeter; but they were defeated and made prisoners by the royal troops. Warbeck was lodged in the Tower of London. He escaped, was retaken, and was hanged. The Mayor of Cork lost his head, and the city of Cork its charter. For many a year afterwards the skulk of those two bold jokers, the Mayor of Cork and his *protegé*, grinned from London Bridge.

A far more accomplished, but scarcely more scrupulous or more fortunate, adventurer, made Cork his home for some years of this period—Sir Walter Raleigh. Sir Walter lived in the suburb we now call Tivoli, where cedars said to have been planted by him still stand. From Cork he wrote some of those wonderful letters, still extant, in which he, a man of twenty-five, seeks, with quaint felicity of style, to persuade Queen Elizabeth, then a maiden of seventy, that he was madly in love with her. Cork was his head-quarters in a long series of military services against the MacCarthys, the Desmonds, the Roches, and the Barrys. Some of these services were notable for knightly valour; others for most unknightly wiles. Thus, at Midleton, then called Chore Abbey, close to where the distillery now stands; he, single-handed, confronted Fitzgerald, Seneschal of Imokilly, with a host, and held the ford until his troops came up. Thus, at Castletown, he disguised himself as a benighted traveller, sought admission to Lord Roche's castle, was hospitably received, and, when supper was over, announced to his host and Lady Roche that they were his prisoners; that their castle was surrounded by his troops; and that they should forthwith be removed to Cork gaol. By such quaint love-making, and such reckless services, he obtained a grant of no less than thirty-six thousand acres of the forfeited Desmond estates. He went to reside at Youghal, where he planted the historical potato. But a quiet country life did not suit so brilliant an adventurer. He left Ireland, sailed for America, discovered Virginia, stormed Guiana, and bore home to England the spoils of many a Spanish galleon. He soon afterwards fell into disgrace, and was imprisoned for ten years in the Tower of London. There he wrote his famous "History of the World". He came back to Cork a ruined man; sold his vast estates for a thousand crowns; and sailed from our harbour on his last desperate venture to seek an Eldorado in the Indies, whence he returned, "broken", as he said, "in brain and heart", to die a traitor's death at Whitehall.

It is another of those "things not generally known," that Cork was also for some years the home of "the poets' poet", the "sage and sweet" Edmund Spencer. Part of the *Faëry Queen* is said to have been written in a lane off the North Main-street. Spencer was sheriff of Cork in 1597. The "Elizabeth" of the "Amoretti" was a country lass from Mallow. The marriage was celebrated in Cork. Thus Spencer bragged to the city belles of his wife's beauty:—

"Tell me, ye merchant daughters, did ye see
So fayre a creature in your town before?
Her goodlie eyes, lyke sapphyres shining bright;
Her forehead ivory white
Her lips lyke cherries, charming men to byte."

Another match-making took place in Cork shortly after Spencer's, and caused more stir. It was that of the Lady Ellen MacCarthy with her kinsman, Florence of Carbery. This match was the subject, not only of local gossip, but of state papers and cabinet councils. The story of it gives some useful insight into the state of society at the time. It is told at full length, and the state papers concerning it are printed, in the valuable *Life of Florence MacCarthy* by Mr. Daniel MacCarthy, published lately by Longman. I can only give a rapid summary.

In the time of Queen Elizabeth, the MacCarthys, though no longer Kings of Cork or of Desmond, were still the greatest family in Munster. Sir Thomas Norms, vice-president of Munster, tells this, in so many words, to Sir Francis Wakingham, the Queen's Secretary of State, in a letter about this very match. "The Clancarties," he says, "are the greatest name and nation in Munster." They owned Desmond, and Carbery, and Muskerry, and Duhallow. They could bring into the field close on five thousand troops. They held a score of castles. Their cadets were lords of Carbery and Muskerry and peers of Parliament. Their chief was the Earl of Clancarthy. Now the Earl's only son, the Baron of Valentia, had lately died. The Earl's only daughter was the Lady Ellen. Young, beautiful, noble, with the dowry of nearly half a county, it is not surprising that her hand was eagerly sought. Its bestowal became a matter of even great political importance. The English authorities resolved that it should be given, as they said, to "some worthy English gentleman". The vice-president of Munster, Sir Thomas Norreys, aspired to it himself; and President Sir Warham St.Leger supported Norrey's suit. But Sir Valentine Brown was more successful, for his son Nicholas. Sir Valentine somehow obtained the recommendation of the Queen herself. He also (having a mortgage of the Earl's estates,) succeeded in getting the formal sanction of the lady's father.

But the lady happened to have a will of her own. She was not disposed to take any "worthy English gentleman". She was in love with her kinsman, Florence MacCarthy; then in attendance at the court of Elizabeth. When, therefore, the Queen's orders arrived, Lady Ellen, with the Countess her mother, so far from rendering implicit obedience to the royal mandate, came boldly to Cork, demanded audience of the Lord-President St. Leger, and protested against it. Why should the Queen coerce a noble maiden's choice? How could the daughter of Clancarthy wed the son of a mere baronet? "Nobilitie of blood" was at least essential. Let some scion "of a noble house" be proposed, and the matter should be considered. The shrewd old Lord-President temporised. He was afraid, as he explained to Wakingham, that "the yonge ladye" would "make off" into O'Ruirk's country. So he assured her that it "stood not with the course of her Majesty's most blessed government" that "any should be forced to marrie against their wills". The ladies took their leave in peace. They said nothing of Florence. Soon afterwards Florence himself arrived in Cork. He waited on the vice-president. He said nothing of the Lady Ellen. He "gave no signe," says Norreys, "of any such purpose as sithence fell out." He even made some complaint against the Earl. He also departed. In a few days afterward tidings reached Cork that Florence and Lady Ellen were married.

Then there was a commotion indeed. Sir Warham St. Leger wrote to the Privy Council. Sir Thomas Norreys wrote to the Secretary of State. Sir William Herbert wrote to Lord Burleigh. A state paper was drawn up "for her Majesty to consider of it". Her Majesty did consider of it. She was not of a temper to be crossed especially in match-making, for which she had a weakness. She ordered the instant arrest of Florence, Lady Ellen, the Countess and all concerned in "this contemptuous action". Sir William

Herbert made himself responsible for the Countess. Florence and his bride were brought to Cork, and spent their honeymoon in Cork gaol. It does not appear, however, to have been a sad honeymoon after all. Sir Valentine Brown wrote a spiteful letter to the Secretary of State, to complain that "at Corcke, Florence, with the Earl's daughter, remayneths with small restraynte, and rather rejoyceth with banquettings than seemeth sorrie". Whereupon Florence was removed to Dublin, and thence to the Tower of London, in which he spent two gloomy years. The "yonge ladye of Clancarthie" was kept in Cork in the custody of " the gentleman porter". Whoever the "gentleman porter" may have been, "the yonge ladye" was too clever for him. One dusky February evening she and her maid, disguised as peasants, slipped out, glided through the city, passed the guard at the South Gate, and sped away into the open country. The authorities were even more indignant than before. The secretary of State wrote to the Lord-President; the Lord-President answered with a doleful apology, still to be read. Nothing was heard of Lady Ellen for many months.

But she reappeared in the most unlikely of all places—the Court of St. James. Thither she had gone to plead her husband's cause before the Queen herself. Elizabeth was not one to be easily moved by beauty or misfortune. Lady Ellen had many a month of weary pleading; many a trial; not a few temptations. Her husband's rents were stayed. Her father's remittances were intercepted. Her suit was laughed at. An inexperienced country lass of twenty, she was left friendless and penniless in a strange capital. Singularly beautiful, heiress of many thousands of broad acres, soon to be a peeress in her own right, she found many to assure her that if she would only give up Florence the most splendid alliances awaited her. Great jurists pronounced that her marriage was invalid. Proceedings for a divorce were ordered. But the true Irish heart never wavered; and keen

Irish wit seconded the true heart's promptings. She won the ear of old Lord Burleigh. Burleigh obtained for her and Florence the Queen's pardon. At length husband and wife returned rejoicing to their home in Carbery. Fair, faithful child of the old race, the annals of a dark and selfish time are brightened by the story of your love and truth, your beauty and your bravery!

What was Cork like at this time? Fortunately, we can tell with some exactness There is a very interesting map of it in the *Pacata Hibernia*. One can recognise the principal objects. One sees how accurate is Spencer's description of Cork as "an island fayre" enclosed by "the spreading Lee" with "his divided flood"; also Camden's contemporary account of Cork, as "of the forme of an egge, with the river flowinge round about it, and runninge between, not passable through but by bridges, lying out at length, as it were, in one direct broad street". That "one direct broad street " corresponds with our North and South Main-streets. It was then called the "Royal-street," sometimes the "High-street", and sometimes the "Queen's Majesty's-street". At either end of it you observe the North and South Gates, with their forts and drawbridges. Crossing it at right angles is Castle-street, through which flowed (as beneath it flows still a branch of the river—"the river flowinge betweene" which Camden observed. At the intersection of Castle-Street and the Main-street, where the Young Men's Society hall now stands, you observe the "Golden Castle" of the Roches. There the Exchange was afterwards built, and for more than a century the trade of Cork was transacted. At the other end of Castle-street, where Daunt's square now is, you will observe "ye Water Gate" and the King and Queen's Castles. To these castles the street owes its name and the city its arms. Ships used to be brought into Castle-street to be unloaded, as at Amsterdam. The custom-house was there to receive them.

The Royal (or Main) street was also intersected then, as it is now, by narrow lanes. These lanes were the fashionable residences of Cork. In them wealthy merchants had their mansions. You see Skiddy's Castle in one and Therry's in another. Spencer, as we noted, lived in one about this very time. Prince Rupert—Cromwell—James II were afterwards entertained in them. You observe Christ Church and St. Peter's, where Christ Church and St. Peter's are still. The former was a castellated church of the Knights Templars. The latter was known as "Oure Ladye Chapelle".

But the most significant object on the map, as it was the chief object of civic care and expenditure, is the great city wall encircling the whole, with the river for a foss, and sixteen towers for a coronal. The eastern walk corresponded with the western side of our present Grand Parade. Portions of them were lately to be seen near Tobin-street. The Marsh, spreading eastward, is the site of the present South Mall, Patrick-street, and the conterminous streets. It looks on the map decidedly like what Lord Macaulay described it—"a desolate marsh, in which a sportsman who pursued the water-fowls sunk deep in the mire at every step". The western wall corresponded with the eastern side of the present Duncan's-street. The river ran here, as depicted on the map, until the close of the last century. To the west were other marshes, on which now stand Nile-street, Henry-street, the Mardyke, &c. This district was called by our fathers, and is still known as, emphatically, "The Marsh". The space inside the walk was scarcely a quarter of a mile in length from north to south, and not more than an eighth of a mile in breadth from east to west.

In the south-west angle of the map are seen the remains of St. Finnbarr's Church, with the significant title, "ye Cathedrale Church of old Corcke". Not far distant from it to the east, at the place we now call Crosses-green, was the Dominican Abbey of St. Mary's of the Isles built on "St.

Dominick's Island" by the Barrys, nearly four centuries before the time we are considering. It had been a famous place. When the Lord-Deputy came to Cork, it was there he lodged. Thence went forth prelates to rule dioceses far and near,—at Cashel of the Kings, in O'Neill's country up north, over in France at fair Toulouse. There died the gallant Edward Mortimer, Earl of March. The abbey, however, had recently been "suppressed" and the image of St. Dominick burned at the high cross of Cork. But popular feeling was too strong for arbitrary power. At the date of which I speak (the close of Elizabeth's reign,) the Friars Preachers were still at their old home; and they held it for nearly a century afterwards. Near this was "the fort of Cork" lately built "to overawe the citizens" of which I shall have more to tell bye-and-bye. Farther east in the southern suburb stood the Augustinian Abbey—"the Red Abbey"—of which I spoke just now, whose tower still stands in Cumberland-street. It is still called the "Red Abbey". Still farther east, where now runs George's-quay, then called the "Red Abbey Marsh" were the Church and Abbey of the Knights of St. John of Jerusalem.

In the north-west suburb, on the North Mall, where North Abbeysquare now stands, was the North Abbey. It was, as you see, actually within arrow-shot of the city walk and North Gate fort. In Elizabeth's time it also, was suppressed. Its rich possessions had been granted to the Skiddys. But there also the friars somehow kept their ground. Farther on to the east, where St. Mary's Church now stands, was Shandon Castle. It was perched on the verge of a precipice, overhanging the river. The adjacent lane is still sometimes known as Shandon Castle-lane. There the Barrys once kept splendid state. There also the Judges of Assize held courts of gaol delivery. Nearly at its foot, just where the Kiln river meets the Lee, was the hamlet of Dungarvan. Close by, where Daly's distillery now stands, was, at the time of which I speak, the Benedictine Convent of St. John. The place is still called John's-street. In 1296 the "Convent Question" was raised about the founding of this convent. Edward I, by royal writ referred to the Chief-Justice of Ireland whether a consent should be established here. The Chief-Justice reported that such an institution would be *ad communem commodum et communam utilitatem totius patriae*; and so the convent was founded and flourished for centuries.

How did the Cork folk live in the sixteenth century? They seem to have been an active, stirring race. Camden tells that Cork was then "a populous little tradinge towne much resorted to". Its "inhabitants," says Hollingshed, were "industrious and opulent". They travelled much, and many foreign merchants resided with them. "Their haven," he truly says, "is an haven roiall." "*Hic etiam cives*," says Stonihurst, "*copius satis locpletes, operam mercaturae navant.*" Dr. Caulfield has published in the *Gentleman's Magazine* a most valuable collection of their wills. These abound with indications of wealth, activity and intelligence. But the characteristic thing about Cork folk during the Norman period is their combination of the martial with the mercantile character. Whether we like to hear it or not, we must never forget that throughout this long Norman time Cork was, simply, an Anglo-Saxon fort and colony on the sea-board of a hostile Irish country. It was, however, a plucky little colony. The mayor and bailiffs, with the advice of the town council, governed the city. They were practically almost independent of external authority. Their edicts had clearly the force of laws. They levied taxes, and regulated commerce. They judged, pilloried, and hanged offenders. They modified the English laws of property. They had a mint and coined their own money, some of which, however, was declared by Act of the English Parliament (16, Edw. IV.) to be "utterly damned". They didn't care much about the Parliament—English or Irish. sometimes they refused to send representatives, and declined to pay any taxes which their representatives had not voted. But they had their troubles both inside the walls and without. Inside they were at constant loggerheads with the soldiery, who came in attendance on the great Anglo-Norman lords that often visited Cork, or the Lord-President of Munster, whose official residence was in Cork. The citizens liked to receive the great lords. In a mercantile view, I suppose their visits were profitable. But their attendants were rollicking, swaggering rascals, whom it was hard to endure. The Bishop of Rosscarbery wrote to the Lord-Justices in October, 1582, a curious complaint about this. He tells their lordships, that "unless these soldiers' insolence be checked, the city people will not stand them". "They esteem," he says, "no more of a mayor than they do of his horse-boy, and their words are these to the best of the town, ' Ye are but beggars and traitors: we are soldiers and gentlemen.'" Outside the walls, the Cork folk had to do almost daily battle with "the Irish enemy". The walls themselves had to be guarded day and night. "The townspeople could not," says Hollinshed, " walk out for recreation," without being " with power of men furnished." But they bore themselves bravely. The greater merchants had castles in the country as well as shops in the town. In the wills that Dr. Caulfield published we find a curious intermixture of castles, town-lands, and the "small wares" of "the shopp". The Roches built Shippool Castle; the Barrys, Shandon and Ballymore Castles. The Sarsfields had a fortress, at Garrycloyne; the Meades at Meadestown; the Martels at Ballymartle. Thus, while the artisan took his turn at defending the walk, the stout burgher-merchant left his counting-house to don his arms and sally out to his castle, at the head of his retainers, like a feudal lord. So they traded, ruled, suffered, and fought, for centuries.

What are we to think of the merits of this long contest? I think they are plain enough. As usual, we must hear both sides. For the annalists at the time were as hot partisans as the soldiers. They smote as hard with their pens as the others with their swords. If you believe the English writers, the Irish were always in the wrong, always treacherous and barbarous, and almost always beaten. If you believe the Irish annalists, The picture was simply reversed; and all the wrong, the treachery, the barbarism, and the beating were on the other side. Nor did it end with this. the literary contest was prolonged after the actual one ceased. The English account got into English literature, and had it to itself, with all its influences, and international communication, for three hundred years. The Irish account has been lately revived with great power, spirit, and effect. The time has come, I think, for considering both impartially. Both contending parties were our ancestors. Both were Irish. after their life-long combat the bones of both have crumbled to dust beneath the same green sod of fatherland.

"Stars, silent, rest o'er us;
Graves, under us silent!"

Speaking in this spirit, then I say that it appears to me, that of both parties, the clash of whose arms scarcely ceased to resound in and about our city for four hundred years, neither was wholly wrong. Each has some right at its side. Each has some claim on our sympathies. Each sustained the struggle with astonishing courage, energy, and endurance. The Celt, and the gallant families that became more Celtic than he, had a clear right to resist invasion. The colonists had no less right to keep what had descended to them, and to fight for their homes and their lives. and, while we heartily sympathise with the grand old race that resisted for centuries the conquerors before whom the greatest nations of the world had yielded, we must admire, too, the proud little city-state, standing out alone for ages in a land of foes, making its own laws, asserting its own rights, extending its trade, and preserving its integrity against all odds all through every emergency.

IV:— HE PENAL PERIOD.
(From 1603 to 1803)

April, 1603, was a stirring month in the stout little City of Cork. The bold burghers were in " a fix". You will remember that for four hundred years previously Cork had been a Norman city warring against the Celts. But it had been this in an isolated, independent sort of way, giving or refusing aid to the Lords of the Pale as seemed to it best—in fact, holding its own against everybody, English, Irish, Spanish, almost like one of those cities of the Hanse, or the Adriatic, with which its merchants were then trading. But now, at the commencement of the 17th century, things had got complicated. The English were stronger; the Celts weaker. Both were tired of strife. Irish princes had accepted English titles; English adventurers were thronging Irish lands. All parties were disposed to compromise. The ancient races, still owning three-fourths of the island, were willing to allow the descendants of the Anglo-Normans to retain what they and their fathers had purchased with their blood, and to join them in all sorts of alliances and intercourse of war and peace. The great Norman families had frankly assented; several of them becoming (as the contemporary English chroniclers complained) "more Irish than the Irish themselves".

It was a reasonable compromise. Every wise nation makes some such. Out of it might have grown a great state homogeneous, happy, and free. But just as the long battle of races had terminated, the long battle of creeds commenced. Stern edicts sped across the Irish seas almost equally unwelcome to both races. The English authorities insisted

24

that Ireland should submit to English rule, not only in temporals but in spirituals. Then up went the sunburst of Tyrone. Then answered the MacCarthy Mors from the south; the O'Moores from the pass of Plumes; the O'Malleys and De Burgos from the western seas. The great rebellion of Tyrone followed. It raged long, and wide, and far. The most splendid army that had ever sailed from an English port had been scattered, like chaff to the winds, by the reckless charge of the Irish chivalry. Don Juan of Spain raised the royal standard of his master above a Spanish fleet and army at Kinsale. The Lord-President of Munster—our poor old wily friend, Sir Warham St. Leger,—was Slain when he ventured a mile outside the gates of Cork.

But then, "the fortune of war" changed. Lord Bacon's sarcasm about the battle of Kinsale was only another version of Hugh O'Neill's bitter complaint, that on this occasion the only difference between Irish and Spanish valour was that "the Irish ran before they were charged; the Spaniards straight after". The O'Neill fought his way desperately back to the north. The MacCarthy More (our friend Florence of Lady Ellen's love,) made such shrewd terms as he well knew how. Don Juan basely bade his lieutenants surrender to the English the O'Sullivans' and O'Driscolls' castles of the sea. The Spanish commander came to Cork and lodged in Portney's-lane. Vain, dull, and fake, beaten in war, humbugged in peace, Don Juan must have been despised by the brave citizens. Still the presence for many weeks of a Spanish Grandee, with his suite, in the little city must have caused a stir. The city belles danced at his balls. But, as the dance sped, the minds of fathers and husbands were perplexed. For here was the difficulty. Cork had supported the Crown against the O'Neill. It hoped thereby to purchase religious freedom for itself. But this was getting doubtful. The penal laws were in full swing in England. They were now being passed upon Ireland, and even on Cork. The very cathedral of Cork had peen appropriated to the changed form of worship. The abbeys, as we have seen, had been suppressed, and I know not by what stratagem their old owners were still kept in them. The City magistracy was still Catholic, and so continued for forty years after; but they were sadly "snubbed" and thwarted by the new Lord-President, Sir George Carew.

And now, in April, 1603, came news of great events. Don Juan had sailed for Spain, to die in not unmerited disgrace. Sir George Carew had sailed for London to report progress to the Queen, or as he said in the high-flown language of the time, "to kiss the shadows of her royal feet". On the 23rd of April it was announced in Cork that Tyrone had submitted to the Queen. On the 4th of May it was announced that the Queen was dead. Then came a week of anxiety. Who was to be king? 'What terms could be made for liberty of conscience? Some spoke of the Infanta of Spain: he would not plunder the old abbeys. Some spoke of the king of the Scots: his mother had died for the old faith. But others said that Spanish insolence could not be brooked and others, again, that James was poor in purse and spirit, and that the President of Munster kept a better table than he.

On the 11th a messenger from Dublin Castle arrived. He was joined by the Lords Commissioners from Shandon Castle. They were received by the Corporation in the Council Chamber. They announced the accession of King James I of England and VI of Scotland, and demanded permission to proclaim him at the High Cross of Cork. The mayor, Thomas Sarsfield, head of the old civic house of the name, enquired what guarantees of freedom of worship would be given by the new king. The commissioners were not instructed on that point: they demanded simply that his Majesty be proclaimed. The mayor, after consultation, stated that the matter was too weighty for an offhand decision, and that by the charter of Cork the council was

entitled to time for consideration. The commissioners represented that the King had already been proclaimed at
Dublin. "So was Perkin Warbeck," said the audacious
mayor. Some one suggested that the mayor might be
committed. "Commit the mayor of Cork!" cried the Recorder, "there is no such power in any here." "Mr. Recorder
ought not break out into a passion," urged suave Mr. Boyle,
the clerk of the council (afterwards "the great Earl of
Cork"). Mr. Recorder answered that he was not in a passion
at all, but that though he was not disposed to "break out"
there were several thousands in Cork sorely tempted to do
so. After many other sharp words, the mayor requested the
commissioners to withdraw to Shandon Castle, and forbade
any of their retinue, or any soldier, inside the city gates.
Then ensued weeks of negotiations, threats, defiances. The
magistrates and nearly all the leading families were in open
rebellion. They would not acknowledge the King unless he
granted freedom of worship. The royal stores were seized.
The New Fort near South Gate, built, as I have said, "to
overawe the citizens," was demolished. Skiddy's Castle
was taken. Shandon Castle was fired at from the walls.
Messenger after messenger came from Dublin without
effect. At length, General Sir Charles Wilmot was dis-
patched with an army to invest the saucy city. But the saucy
city would not even be invested. The mayor would not let
Sir Charles enter with more than six soldiers, and forbade
the army to lodge in the suburbs. The King's general
thought fit to comply with the mayor's orders, and withdrew
to Youghal. It was evident that the stout burghers, who so
often held the walls against threat Irish lords, might hold it
against an English general too.

On Easter day a letter arrived from the Lord Deputy,
commanding submission. The mayor and recorder again
declined, unless liberty of worship were conceded.

It was not until the night of the 10th of May, when the Lord Deputy, in person, appeared with an army at North Gate, that the Cork men were disposed to yield. Even then the Deputy and his army were bidden to wait for a day outside the walls, while the council deliberated. Their deliberation was long; their debate vehement. The memorable division list is still to be read. The Sarsfields, Meades, Terrys, Goulds, Fagans, Morroghs were for holding out. The Coppingers, Gallways, Martells, Roches, were for more prudent council. These latter prevailed. The Lord-Deputy was admitted on the following day. But terms must have been made; for Sarsfield continued in office, and almost the only victim was one poor bragging Lieutenant Morrogh, who had called General Wilmot a traitor, and challenged him to disprove it in single combat. Thus began and ended "Tom Sarsfield's rebellion".

For a generation afterwards the great civic families —Sarsfields, Meades, Roches, Gallways, Goulds, Fagans, Therrys, Morroghs &..,—remained Catholic, retained the civic magistracy, and struggled hard for freedom of worship. But they fought what was then a losing fight. The Lord-Presidents and their adherents yearly increased in Power. Thus, within three years of Sarsfield's rebellion, another Sarsfield, then mayor, was sent to gaol and fined five hundred pounds for going to mass. In fact, the whole weight of English influence and English law was against the old citizens. "Queen Jamie," as even courtiers called the king, was forced to declare from the throne that he "would not tolerate" any profession of his mother's creed; and he "planted" Ulster, as we know. Then came Charles's turbulent times and Strafford's iron rule. Freedom from worship was promised as "a grace" if certain Moines were given by the Catholics to the Crown. The wealthy traders of Cork eagerly subscribed. Alderman Dominick Roche gave two thousand pounds. Strafford took the money and refused the "grace". Soon afterwards he paid the penalty, not only of his crimes but of his virtues, with his head. Things grew worse in Cork as elsewhere. At length the Catholics of the English interest (those of Cork included,) united with the Catholics of the Irish interest in the Confederation of Kilkenny, and declared "PRO REGE, PRO FIDE, ET PRO PATRIA" —for the king, for the faith, and for the country.

At this time Sir Robert Coppinger was mayor of Cork. He was a staunch Catholic and an enthusiastic Royalist. Through the intervention of one "Father Mathew" (how curiously the name sounds in this connection!) he had arranged with the Confederation that the King's General, Mac Carthy, Lord Muskerry, should take possession of Cork. Muskerry was on his march, when the plot was baffled by a counterplot so striking in its circumstances that no story of our civic history would be complete without it. The hero of this latter plot was Captain Muschamp, governor of the Fort of Cork—that same fort, "close to the South Gate" which Mayor Sarsfield had demolished, but which had since been rebuilt "to overawe the citizens". Muschamp was a Parliamentarian, and had resolved to hand over Cork to the King's enemies. Now it happened that one hot July evening in this year (1644) Captain Muschamp went out for a walk. He strolled into the city. As he passed South Gate fort, it was observed that the gallant captain was, what men would now call, "screwed". But, as I suppose, there was nothing unusual in this, he was allowed to pass. He "toddled on" to the mayor's house. "Master Mayor" was at home. Some of the leading magistrates were dining with him. The captain, "being in a merry humour," invited himself to join them. Sir Robert hospitably assented. Muschamp was, "after the Irish fashion, kindly entertained". "Divers cups," says the chronicler, "of sack, claret, and usquebaugh passed round to welcome him." "Sitting at dinner," the chronicler goes on to say, "they discoursed of the distractions of the time." Opinions differing, and usquebaugh being strong, the argument grew warm. At length the captain insolently said that he was against the King whose coat he wore, and that if the citizens did not "take the covenant" he would with "the great ordnance in the fort, beat down all the houses in Cork about their ears". This was too much. The magistrates rose. They said he had spoken treason, and should answer for it. They ordered his arrest. He was brought before the governor. The governor complimented the magistrates on their loyalty, lamented that an officer in such trust should so commit himself, and arranged for his trial by court-martial. In a few days Muschamp was tried, found guilty, and sentenced to be hanged outside the walls at Gallows-green. The governor invited the mayor, magistrates and leading citizens to be present at the execution. Accordingly, at the appointed time, the prisoner was brought forth to die. The mayor, the sheriffs, the principal merchants, and the city guard of musketeers attended. Few persons of any rank remained within the walls. All streamed out through the South Gate, passed the fort, on to Gallows-green. But here the scene changed. Captain Muschamp was set at liberty. The mayor, the sheriffs, the magistrates, and "all the chiefest citizens" were seized, and hustled off to prison in the fort hard by. Muschamp took possession of the city gates, raised the drawbridges, refused re-admission to the city guard and to the citizens became, in fact, master of Cork. The disaster was complete and irretrievable. A list of over two hundred "chiefest citizens" thus expelled is extant. It includes all the old civic names, commencing with Sir Robert Coppinger and David Sarsfield, Lord Kilmallock. Subsequently a few were allowed to return, on condition of taking the covenant and renouncing their faith. But the vast majority preferred to wander off houseless, homeless, landless. They deposited the city mace and other civic insignia with the Lord Lieutenant. There was no mayor of Cork for ten years afterwards, and no Catholic mayor for two hundred years; when, in our own times, Sir Thomas Lyons reached the civic chair.

An interesting illustration of this expulsion of the citizens occurs in *De la Boullaye Le Gouz Travels*, published at Paris nine years afterwards. The writer relates how he made the acquaintance of a young Cork gentleman whom he designates "Tam Neuel," but who I suppose, would have called himself Tom Neville. He befriended "Tam," and lent him money. In return "Tam" invited him on a visit to his father's house at "Korq". M. Le Gouz assented. They arrived in Cork in 1644. But a grievous disappointment awaited them. "Tam" knocked at his father's door. A stranger opened it. "Tam" asked for his father. No such person lived there. "Tam" pressed his enquiries. The stranger recollected that he had heard of some such person as having lived in that house, but that the previous year he had been expelled with the rest of the Catholic inhabitants. Poor "Tam!" I suppose some hot tears fell on the old threshold. But "Tam" discovered a relative who hospitably entertained his French acquaintance, and repaid what Tom had borrowed. "Tam's" father had gone to Spain, having lost ten thousand pounds by the expulsion. The sight which most struck Le Gouz in Cork, was "*le Puits des Dimanche*" or, as he himself translates it, "The Well of Sunday". Our corporate authorities have taken care that "The Well of Sunday " shall not distract the attention of tourists any more. The old tablet on its front bears the date of Le Gouz' visit. there is little vestige of the "fountain's fairybrim" which "Father Prout" celebrated two centuries afterwards.

Many of the old citizens must have returned to Cork three years after, when William O'Brien, Lord Inchiquin, the Parliamentarian general under whom Captain Muschamp acted, changed his own colours, and declared for King Charles. Inchiquin was himself a striking specimen of the brilliant, gallant, unscrupulous soldier of fortune, characteristic of the age. He had fought in Catalonia against the Algerines. He had governed Morocco for the king. He had defeated the King's troops a dozen times during the recent Irish war. Last time it was at Knockanoss, to the west of Mallow. There he routed a royal army under Lord Taaffe, and put to the sword the gallant Sir Alexander McAllister, the hero of "McAllister's march". On the news of the victory, Parliament voted him its thanks, and a present of a thousand pounds. His acknowledgement was to declare against the Parliament. He seized Cork for the King. He invited thither the Marquis of Ormond, the King's commander-in-chief. It was in Cork, in September, 1684, that Lord Ormond made that famous treaty of peace with the Confederation of Kilkenny, which, because of its stipulation that ten thousand Irish troops should go to help the King in England, had to be disclaimed by the unfortunate monarch, then a prisoner in the Isle of Wight; and was one of the "articles of impeachment" for which, in four months afterwards, he laid his weary head upon the block at Whitehall.

The news of the King's execution struck the world with amazement. No such event had ever yet occurred in Europe's history. Few, I suppose, were more astonished than the officers of the King's fleet, then lying at Kinsale, in command of the gallant Prince Rupert, who was not only one of the first cavalry officers, but one of the first naval commanders of his time. They sent into mourning, displayed black ensigns, and proclaimed King Charles II. But their mourning was cut short by the blockade of Admiral Blake, with nearly all the navy of the Commonwealth. Rupert for once was cautious, and, instead of seeking to break the blockade, lay by in the harbour until the winter storms drove off the enemy. But meantime the royal fleet was half-starved. It was to seek for provisions for his men that the haughtiest prince in Europe came to the city of Cork. Picture to yourselves the fiery little man, draped in black, with his suite of cavalry captains improvised into naval officers, supplicating the citizens for bread and meat. I am glad to say he did not supplicate in vain. Large supplies left South Gate for the half-starved sailors at Kinsale. It was characteristic of Rupert that he also asked for fire ships to burn off the enemy. But these the Cork folks would not or could not supply.

One dark night in November after Prince Rupert's visit there was another change of scene on our little stage. It occurred dramatically. Sir Robert Starling, the Royalist governor, lay fast asleep. So lay nearly every one else in the island city. But not so Colonel Jeffryes. Jeffryes and a few staunch fellows were in command of "ye Water Gate"—the gate which stood at the end of Castle-street. Jeffryes opened the gate, and peered out into the bleak, watery marsh which is now St. Patrick-street. Soon came plashing footsteps. and then, knee or waist deep in the cold slush, a troop of soldiers; and then another troop; and still others, until five hundred had arrived, and had mustered within the gate. They were picked troops of the Commonwealth, sent by Cromwell to seize Cork. Their commander was Colonel Phair, one of Cromwell's most trusted officers —the same to whom, ten months before, the execution of the King's death-warrant had been confided. Then ensued what Carlyle describes as an "universal hurly-burly". In "Lady Fanshawe's Memories" we get a vivid account of it. Lady Fanshawe was the wife of a royalist officer. She was living outside the city, at the Red Abbey, whose tower in Cumberland-street we know so well. Her husband had gone to Kinsale that day. At midnight she "heard the great guns go off" and soon afterwards "lamentable shrieks of men, women, and children". She dressed hurriedly. She raised the window. She saw, in swift, sorrowful flight, crowds of citizens, "stripped and wounded, and turned out of the town". Inquiring the cause, she was informed that Colonel Jeffreys had seized Cork for Cromwell. Then followed three long hours of suspense. What to do? The plucky little woman decided. She wrote a letter to her husband, and sent it by a messenger who was "let down the garden wall of the Red Abbey," and "sheltered by the darkness," escaped. Then at three o'clock that bleak November morning, taper in hand, she went out. She passed an " unruly tumult with swords in their hands". She threaded her way to "the market-place." She sought and found Colonel Jeffryes. She reminded him of the "many civilities" he had received from her husband. Jeffryes responded to the appeal, and "instantly wrote" her " a pass". With this she "returned through thousands of naked swords to the Red Abbey". She there "hired a neighbour's cart" and with a few trembling servants, her sister, and her " little girl, Nan" got safely off to Kinsale. In another memoir of the time, written by one of Phair's officers, are found some grim Cromwellian jokes about this seizure of Cork: how Governor Starling "little dreamed of losing his command, and yet found he had lost when he waked, so that it might be truly said he was taken napping" and how it might be urged in his defence that "as he was divested of his government in the dark, he could not reasonably be expected to see to prevent it".

A fortnight afterwards there leaped, as it were on our little stage, bloody sword in hand, the greatest captain of his age—one of the greatest captains of any age—who "never fought a battle without gaining it;" "who never gained a battle without annihilating the force opposed to him;" " terrible as Death, relentless as Doom;" red with the blood of Drogheda and Wexford—the Lord Lieutenant of Ireland, the Lord General of England, OLIVER CROMWELL! With him came, thronging every house in city and suburb, fifteen thousand "Roundheads"—those grim soldier-fanatics who never feared a foe and never spared a victim, with their watchword: "Cursed be he that holdeth back his sword from blood; yea, cursed be he that maketh not his sword stark drunk with Irish blood!" They made a gloomy Christmas of it in Cork, in 1649. From Cork, Cromwell, directed operations against the neighbouring fortresses. Here he indicted what Carlyle considers "the remarkablest state paper ever published in Ireland". Here he wrote his report of the victory over Lord Ormond, which received the thanks of the Parliament. "This letter," observes Carlyle, "though dated Cork, 19th December, did not reach London until the 8th January, so great were the delays of the winter post." The celebrated Protestant Bishop Bramhall, *protegé* of stern Strafford, friend of gentle Jeremy Taylor, was in Cork at this time, and narrowly escaped him. "I would have given a good sum," said Cromwell "for that Irish Canterbury!" Cromwell ordered the church bells of Cork to be converted into battering ordnance; and when remonstrated with, replied, that "as gunpowder was invented by a priest, it was not amiss to promote their bells into cannons". He made a grimmer joke still on Richard Magner, of Castle Magner, near Mallow. Magner waited on him, and was favourably received. At his departure, Cromwell requested him to take a letter to Colonel Phair. Magner galloped off on his errand. But on his way he was tempted to open the letter. He did not deem himself bound to proceed with it when he found it contained the terse instruction: "Execute the bearer.—O.C." Cromwell's lieutenant, Lord Broghill, seems to have imbibed some of his leader's spirit. Besieging Macroom about this time, he brought Bishop MacEgan, of Ross, then his prisoner, to the walls, to exhort the besieged to surrender. "Hold out to the last!" cried the bishop. A true soldier would have honoured this heroism which in Regulus has won the applause of all succeeding ages. But Broghill hanged the prelate on the next tree.

In his distribution of forfeited property Cromwell was not unmindful of his personal friends. Amongst these was Admiral William Penn. In 1664 Cromwell wrote to Ireland to direct that the admiral should have lands to the value of £300 in the County of Cork, near some fortified place. The place selected was that same Castle and Manor of Macroom which Broghill had seized for the commonwealth. The admiral got them, and lived at Macroom for some years. But the Castle and Manor of Macroom happened to be the property of the Royalist General, Mac Carthy, Lord Muskerry, of whom I spoke a while ago. On the accession of Charles II, MacCarthy, more fortunate than most other Irish royalists of the time, got back his titles and most of his lands—amongst others, those which Cromwell had given Penn. As an equivalent, Penn got the castle and lands of Shanagarry, near Cloyne. His descendants still possess these lands. In 1667 the admiral, being living in London, sent his son William, then in his twenty-fourth year, and an attache of the Viceregal Court, to take charge of his estate. Young William Penn accordingly lived in the city of Cork for two or three years. It is a pleasing illustration of his mild and kindly character, that he let the lands to the former tenants on long leases, at rent so moderate as to bring a remonstrance from the old admiral. While in Cork, Penn met a college friend, Thomas Lee, who had settled here as a minister of the recently-established Society of Friends. Their intimacy resulted in Penn's becoming, as they say, a Quaker. But the Quakers, like the Catholics, were then the victims of persecution. That very year Lord Orrery had called the attention of the Mayor of Cork to the "conventicles" in the city and suburbs, and directed all who attended them to be seized and punished. On the 3rd September afterwards, Penn and his friends, while meeting in some such "conventicle" were apprehended and brought before the mayor. The mayor, out of respect for Penn's rank, offered to release him upon his giving a bond not to commit a similar infraction of the law. This Penn manfully refused. Thus it happened that the future founder of Pennsylvania spent a month as a prisoner in the common gaol of Cork. He was released by Lord Orrery, to whom he had written a spirited and characteristic appeal. "Religion," said Penn "which is at once my crime and mine innocence, makes me a prisoner to a mayor's malice, but a free man to myself."

On his release he returned to his father's house in London. But soon after, having refused to take off his hat to the King, he was turned out of doors by the choleric old admiral. He then became a minister of the persuasion he had embraced in Cork, and of which he rose to be the most illustrious leader and champion. The Society of Friends were only strengthened by Lord Orrery's persecution, and have been ever since, as they are now, amongst the most prosperous, the most kindly, and the most high-minded of the citizens of Cork.

But though the persecution of the Society of Friends was happily abated, that of the Roman Catholics was cruelly continued until the death of Charles II. Thus, in 1664, a noble and venerable lady, the Viscountess Fermoy, was publicly hanged at Gallows-green. In 1666 all Roman Catholics were ordered to leave the city. In 1670 the celebration of Catholic worship was forbidden. In 1680, the Catholic Bishop of Cork, Dr. Creagh, was tried for his life, and only saved by the accident of the courthouse falling—nearly every one in it but the bishop being killed or wounded. In 1682, all Catholics above the rank of artisans were ordered out of the city. Their Protestant fellow-citizens scrupulously complied with the royal proclamation by putting them out; but they promptly obeyed a higher law by immediately letting them in again.

With the accession of James II, the tide of Cork affairs turned once more, there arrived here as Lord-President and

Commander-in-chief of Munster, a descendant of the Celtic kings of Cork, General Justin Mac Carthy. General Mac Carthy was a younger son of that Lord Muskerry whom Captain Muschamp outwitted, a slice of whose lands Cromwell gave to Admiral Penn. He was nephew of the Duke of Ormond. He had married a daughter of the celebrated Lord Strafford. His eldest brother, Lord Muskerry, who is mentioned in King James's Memoirs as a distinguished officer, had fallen by James's side in the great seafight of Southhold Bay, and had been interred with great pomp in Westminster Abbey. The then Lord Clancarty was his nephew, and had been married under his auspices to Lady Spencer, daughter of the Earl of Sutherland. General Mac Carthy had served with distinction in the French army. He was then a British general. Nearly all accounts represent him as one of the most gallant officers, and at the same time, one of the most honest and kindly gentlemen, of his day.

In Cork at all events he was gallant, honest, and kindly. Catholics, under his auspices, were, of course, invited to return to their homes; but no Protestants were allowed to be expelled. Catholics were readmitted to the franchise; but no Protestant was disfranchised. He allowed the local magistracy to remain in Protestant hands. Arms and horses had to be seized to prevent rebellion; but the owners were compensated, and outrages prohibited. When Dominick Terry's house at the Red Abbey was plundered by some of Mac Carthy's soldiers, the plunderers were punished, and the house restored. When in some gust of popular feeling some Protestant citizens were turned out of the city, they had only to appeal to General Mac Carthy or his kindly lieutenant, Sir James Cotter, to be reinstated. Long years afterwards the Protestants of Cork bore earnest official testimony, under the hands and seals of their mayor and sheriffs, that under Mac Carthy's rule they had been treated with "civilitie" with "humanity and kindness" and, in fact, "did receive all manner of countenance".

But, nevertheless, it was a stern time; and Mac Carthy had stern work to do. Bandon revolted, and murdered its Royalist garrison. The President marched on the town. On his approach the Bandonites craved pardon, and opened their gates. He let them off with a fine of one thousand pounds and the demolition of their walls, never since rebuilt. He was officially reprimanded for his clemency. But soon after he was raised to the peerage as Viscount Mountcashel.

He did not enjoy his new honours many months when he encountered an overwhelming disaster. Despatched to the North against the gallant "Protestant Boys" of Enniskillen, his raw levies were utterly routed in the great battle of Newtownbutler. Deserted by his troops, he scorned to flee. With a few faithful followers he rushed into the midst of his pursuers, was desperately wounded in several places, and nearly found the death he sought. But he was recognised, spared, and made prisoner. As prisoner he was treated with kindness. He is accused of effecting his escape by a breach of parole; and the great authority of Lord Macaulay sanctions the charge. As, however, he was acquitted by a jury of officers, and as friends and foes acknowledge him to be a man of honour, I think we may acquit him too.

After his escape he paid Cork a brief visit. Wounded, defeated, accused of dishonour, it is not wonderful that he availed of the first opportunity to return to France. There he founded the famous Irish Brigade. He commanded it for ten years. It was called after him "Mountcashel's Brigades". His subsequent exploits make part of European history. In Germany, in Piedmont, and in the Alps, he made Europe ring with the narratives of his splendid valour. To this day, the tourist to Italy by the Mount Cenis route, is shown a gorge of the Graian Alps, where "my lor Moncassel" defeated the army of Piedmont, and took its commander prisoner. There, too, we get a last glimpse of the old gentleness, and, at the same time, a curious confirmation of an historical fact. We find Mountcashel entertaining his prisoner, the Count de la Salle, at his own table. Talk turns on the Irish King Dathy, who, twelve hundred years before, was said to have pushed his victories to the Alps. De la Salle mentions that, in the archives of his own family, it is stated that an Irish monarch of that name had lodged twelve hundred years before in the Chateau de la Salle, in the Savoyard Alps. But, while the kindly host was chatting with his guest about the far past, he was himself dying. He expired at Barege a few weeks afterwards. You can see his portrait in this city, painted by Sir Peter Lely. It belongs to his relatives, the MacCarthys of Carrignavar. Sir Lely died in 1690, it must have been painted while Lord Mountcashel was a young man. It is, indeed, quite a youthful figure. At first one is only struck by its girlish fairness of face and litheness of frame. It certainly indicates gentleness and kindness. But, inspected more closely, you discover in the firm lips, the proud nostril, and the gallant "pose" some suggestions of the dauntless soldier of Newtownbutler, Embrun, and Isere.

The French fleet that bore Lord Mountcashel to France had brought the last of the Stuart kings to Kinsale. Almost immediately afterwards, James II arrived in Cork. He remained here for a fortnight, just one hundred and eighty years ago. He lodged at first in Dominick Roche's lane—as Tobin-street was then called, afterwards with the Dominican friars, in the old Abbey of St. Mary's, (which somehow they had up to that time retained) at Crosses-green. He attended mass in royal state at the North Abbey. He received the Lord-Lieutenant and the great officers of the kingdom at Shandon Castle. His fleet, six-and-thirty sail of the line, rode in Cork harbour. Eight regiments of King Louis' army thronged the little city, as Cromwell's Round-heads had thronged it a generation before. What hopes, what fears, must have throbbed in the breasts of Cork folk in that anxious march of 1689!

James left Cork, as he had left many another place, a legacy of sorrow and shame. He reversed the kindly rule of Mac Carthy. He superseded MacCarthy's governor, Sir James Cotter. In their places he appointed the stern Lord Clare and the greedy Antoine Boileau. For eighteen months the Protestants of Cork were shamefully persecuted. Some, like Mayor Crone, hurried off to their gallant brethren at Londonderry. Others, like Dean Davies, took ship for England. Many were imprisoned. Many were sent off to neighbouring towns. Many more were robbed. Boileau is said to have sent to France several thousands of pounds, the proceeds of the plunder of a city which had somehow until then, through all its changes, contrived to be prosperous. Bishop Creagh, one is glad to find, protested against this iniquity; but he was answered only by a ribald jest. The Protestants appealed to the courts of law, and they were told from the bench at Cork, by the Chief-Justice of the highest criminal court of the realm, that robbery, at that juncture, must be tolerated as a necessary evil.

Meantime the Boyne was lost and won. King " James the Coward" had fled and, in November, 1690, King William's fleet bore into Cork Harbour. Soon afterwards the Duke of Wurtemburg was thundering from Shandon Castle at the North, and the famous Churchill (soon to be Duke of Marlborough, conqueror of Ramilies, Blenheim, and Malplaquet) was preparing for his first siege on the heights which command the city at the south. The old walls were useless against modern artillery. The hills commanding the city would have made any walls ineffectual. Dr. Caulfield has edited, with rare learning, the journal of an eye-witness—the martial Dean Davies. Indeed the Dean seems to have been worth any captain present. His local knowledge suggested various routes. He brought the Wurtemburg soldiers round by Carrigrohan. He cut off the water supply from Droupes's mills. Hs suggested how to silence the firing from the fort at the south—the same Elizabeth Fort of Muschamp's days, whose stout walls still tower over Barrack-street. He utilised old St. Finnbarr's Round Tower, near the cathedral, which had stood until then. Captain Horatio Townsend got to the top of it with two guns and two files of men. The fort answered with a thundering volley, which shook the tower to its base. The men wanted to get down, but Captain Townsend ordered the ladders to be removed, and held his post until the fort surrendered. The most striking incident of that famous siege was the fall of the brave young Duke of Grafton, struck by a ball from the ramparts, as he advanced at the head of his regiment, up to his shoulders in water, across " the Rape Marsh," now the South Mall. You know the place where he fell is still called Grafton's Alley. On Michaelmas Day, 1690, after a gallant resistance, Cork surrendered.

Cork folk have seen some tragic sights, but none, I think, more sorrowful than that which, in the November following, was presented on the quays of Cork. It was the departure for France of Sarsfield and the heroic defenders of Limerick. The conditions of their capitulation were twofold: a free transit to France for themselves and families, and freedom of worship for their fellow-countrymen. The imperfect fulfilment of the first condition gave them a bitter foretaste of the shameful violation of the second. Twelve thousand men, with their wives and families, arrived in Cork for embarkation. At best their condition was sorrowful. It was a bleak November time. It was a stern Williamite city. They were beaten men. The gallant fight had failed. Many were desperately wounded; many sick; all broken in fortune. Before them was a wintry voyage, a strange country, an uncertain future. Around them were trembling wives and half-famished children. But, at the last moment, came a disappointment sufficient to wring a cry of agony from the stoutest heart alive. The accommodation provided for their transit was utterly imperfect and inadequate. The first ship was scarcely filled when it blew up, showering the mangled limbs of men, women, and children on their comrades. But this was not all, or the worst. After the soldiers had been embarked in the other ships, it turned out that there was no room for the women and children. Sarsfield protested. Some room was made. Many got on board. The ships were crammed perilously. But still a great multitude remained. As the last boats put off, there was a rush into the surf. Some women caught hold of the ropes, were dragged out of their depth, clung till their fingers were cut through, and perished in the waves. The ships begun to move. A wild and terrible wail arose from the shore. It was echoed from the ships. But wailing was in vain. The ships sped on. The women and children were left behind.

It is pleasant to read that the Protestant and Williamite Cork-folk, again kinder than their rulers or their laws, compassionated and succoured the unwillingly forsaken. The brave exiles soon sent for their kith and kin. The gloom of that dark day was forgotten in the splendour of many a foreign city, court, and camp. "One of these exiles," says Lord Macaulay, "became a marshal of France. Another became Prime Minister of Spain. In his palace at Madrid he had the pleasure of being assiduously courted by the ambassador of George II, and bidding defiance, in high terms, to the ambassador of George III. Scattered over all Europe, they were soon to be found brave Irish generals, dextrous Irish diplomatists, Irish counts, Irish barons, Irish knights of St. Lewis and St. Leopold, of the White Eagle and the Golden Fleece, who, if they had remained in the house of bondage, could not have been ensigns of marching regiments, or freemen of petty corporations."

Let us now pause for a little and look at Cork in 1690, as a contemporary map reveals it. Compared with the map of nearly a hundred years before, there is not much evidence of progress. The suburbs have been a good deal extended north and south, and the eastern marshes have been partially drained. A bowling-green has been made near the place where Bowling Green Street now is. But the city proper was still limited to the old fortified islands. All outside these, except the northern and southern mainlands, was mere marsh or "slob". St. Patrick-street, the Parade, the South Mall, George's-street, Duncan-street, Henry-street, Nile-street, as yet were not. The intramural and suburban castles had almost disappeared. The fortified walls, were also fast disappearing. Marlborough's cannon had made several breeches. The citizens made several gateways. In two years after the date of this map, "the mayor, sheriffs, and com-monalty of his Majesty's ever loyal city of Cork" petitioned the Lord Lieutenant for liberty to open gates, in the walls, and to discontinue their maintenance, inasmuch as the tide ebbs and flowed around them, and the ground beyond them might be useful. This permission was given. The corpora-tion made leases of the outlying tracts at low rents to enterprising citizens. These tracts were called by the names of the lessees. Thus the Grand Parade was afterwards built on "Dunscombe's Marsh," and the Mansion House on Hammond's Marsh".

For a century afterwards Cork languished under the Penal Laws. We have seen how boldly the old Cork families struggled for religious liberty. We have seen how the defenders of Limerick made it an article of the famous treaty. King William III wished to observe that treaty. He was not a man for heroic sacrifices for honour or justice; but his nature was just and tolerant; his mind was expanded by intercourse with many men of many creeds and nations. It was not without a struggle he allowed himself to become the tool of a persecuting faction. At first he let Catholics worship free. He granted pardons by hundreds. He reversed forfeitures by scores. He rebuked some Cork zealots for intolerance. His bosom-friend, Lord Sydney, received at Dublin Castle the Catholic Bishop of Cork. But passion and faction were too strong for statesmanship and good faith. Sydney had to be re-called. The king himself was threatened. The Penal Laws were passed. In 1704 there were but four priests in Cork. Catholics were excluded from all magistracies and all professions. They could not be members of parliament or vote for members of parliament. They could not be members of a corporation, or vote for any such members. They could not take leases for longer than thirty-one years. They could not improve lands so as to yield a profit equal to a third of the rents. If any Catholic bought any land, any Protestant could seize it. If any Catholic had a horse worth more than £5, any Protestant might tender £5, and take it. For any Catholic to keep school was banishment; to return, death. A Catholic child could not go to school at home, or go abroad to be educated. A Catholic son becoming Protestant, became entitled to the reversion of his father's lands. A Catholic wife becoming Protestant, became guardian of the children. To teach Catholics was felony. To be a Catholic bishop, transportation. For a Catholic Bishop to return after transportation, death. The system was designed, as Burke points out, "for the oppression, impoverishment, and degradation of a people". To a great extent it succeeded. There was an almost complete revolution of property and of social status. To bear an Irish surname became a mark of inferior station. In order to be an aristocrat in rank it was necessary to be a *parvenu* in race. It was not "respectable" to adhere to the creed of nearly every prince in Christendom. Only three Roman Catholic families in the county of Cork retained their estates, and these only by the protection of their Protestant friends. Of course Cork languished under this vile code. As mercy is twice blessed, persecution is twice accursed: cursing those that inflict and those that endure. "The thriving little tradinge towne" of a hundred years before became poor and idle. Its commerce fell away. Its woollen trade was ruined. Dean Swift tells us that, in his time, "Cork, which had been a few years before a place of trade, has gone to decay and the wretched merchants have becom. mere pedlars." I do not detain you for any malediction on the Penal Laws. I might quote a column of splendid denunciations from the greatest writers of our language; but really the mere mention of such laws is enough. Your own generous hearts, your own clear heads denounce them as I read. "The code," says the late Professor of History at Oxford "stands in need of all the palliations which the largest and calmest view of history can afford and when all these palliations have been exhausted, its memory will still remain a reproach to human nature, and a terrible monument of the vileness into which nations may be led when their religion has been turned into hatred, and they have been taught to believe that the indulgence of the most malignant passions of man is an acceptable offering to God."

Let us pause again, and see how Cork looked in the middle of the last century, as Smith's map and "view" reveal it. The city walls have almost disappeared. The marshes have been mapped out into streets. The river, or "dock," as it was called, runs through Patrick-street. In the "view" you see the ships in it, and the drawbridge crossing near where the Mathew statue now is. Drawbridge-street still retains the name, and verifies the position of this bridge. Houses have been built on the marshy islands. The King's Castle still remains in Castle-street. Castle-street is connected with what we now call the Grand Parade by a bridge. At the other end is another bridge, connecting Tuckey-street (or quay, as it was called) with the Grand Parade. It was on this bridge

"George ahorseback" flourished for a generation. Tuckey's-quay had been a piece of waste ground outside the city walls, but was built on when the walls were torn down. Patrick's-bridge was not built for forty years afterwards. Merchants'-quay you see, bears the singular name of "Cold Harbour". Lavitt's-quay was called "Sevenovens-quay," (after a merchant named Sevenovens) as if in anticipation of the Refreshment Company's establishment. To the west you observe the Assemblyrooms. The bowling-green had been transferred thither from Dunscombe's Marsh. A good Dutchman, Edward Webber by name, emulating his native boulevards, laid out "the Mardyke" at his own expense; and peace be with him for it! You observe the dear and familiar, though not exquisitely graceful, contour of Shandon steeple. It was built in 1720, out of the ruins of the old Shandon Castle, of which I spoke so often. The stone must have run short; for two sides of the steeple are of red sandstone, two of white limestone. Hence Father Prout's couplet—

"Partsy-coloured, like the people,
Red and white, stands Shandon steeple."

Christ Church steeple had been taken down because It leaned over like the tower at Pisa; yet it left us for over a century the proverb: "all a-one-side, like Christ Church". You recognise the "Mall Isle" as the commencement of the South Mall. You see St. Finnbarr's in the distance. Lastly, you notice, both in map and view the Cork Institution, then known as the new custom-house. It was built in 1724, and continued be be used as a custom-house until 1803. You will observe how conveniently "the dock" ran up to its door, over the space we now call Nelson's-place.

In 1768 there were no public lamps whatever in Cork, except one on the drawbridge. In 1769 rioting was so common in Cork, that it was not safe for any person to stand at his own door without some weapon of defence. The docks and quays being unfenced, accidents were of daily occurrence. Vast numbers of voracious pigs infested the streets, so that the mayor had to plant pig-traps at various points. Noxious effluvia were emitted from the marshes when the tidal waters receded. Even "the wholesome northern blasts" were corrupted, as Dr. Rogers complained in 1734, by the "great slaughter-houses on the Glanmire hills".

Considering the decline of commerce, the ruin of trade, the rioting, the darkness, the effluvia, the slaughter-houses, the pigs, and the Penal Laws, our fathers must have had "hard times" of it a hundred years ago. It was, I think, the very gloomiest period of our civic history. But henceforth things improved. In Cork, earlier than in most places, the good feeling of the Protestant community itself revolted against the baseness of the penal code, and practically released its most obnoxious provisions. Nearly every local lawyer has met instances in which land was bought in Protestant names, and preserved with rigid honour for the Catholic proprietors. The proscription of priests and bishops was gradually allowed to become inoperative. The North and South Chapels were built. The Friars were allowed to open modest chapels in various lanes. Catholics got into trade, and acquired wealth. Their continental connections proved serviceable for mercantile purposes. Our chief export trades in beef and butter were thus founded. "Alexander, the Coppersmith" a rabid pamphleteer of the time, gives curious, because unwilling, testimony to this mercantile progress. He divides the "religion of Cork" into "Episcopacy, Presbyterianism, Quakerism, Anabaptism, Hugounotism, Hypocrisy, and—Popery!" Of course the Papists are the worst of any. He protests against "their impudence, running openly into every branch of trade, talking big upon change, and importing the cargoes of priests who swarm about the city". He predicts that their "bold monopoly of home and foreign trade" will raise such a clamour that the law must interfere. He complains that "the trade of the city has been forced from its natural course into another channel, within a few years; that the most considerable branch of our trade has been the export of great quantities of beef to our plantations, to supply the French; but that now the French galleys come hither themselves, always consigned to a Popish factor, whose relations and correspondence," he continues, "are abroad and at home; whose diligence being more, and luxury less, than the Protestants, will, at last, swallow up the trade, and suck the marrow of the city, and, like the ivy, will grow up to be an oak, and will prove absolute in their power over the commerce of those on whom they should have depended for bread; and," he proceeds, waxing passionate, "how secure do men of that religion live in despite of the law, whilst Protestants look idly on—and suspend the operation of laws which never required, no not at their first making—a more severe execution than at this day". By running away with this profitable branch, not only the prejudice they do a Protestant trader, but the benefit arising to Popish dealers and tradesmen, is destructive of the Protestant interest of the city. From the mutual kindness of all men under oppression, and a natural hatred of their oppressors, they deal with, and always employ one another. "If," he declares, in a paroxysm of indignation, "a Papist at the gallows" (at Gallows-green) "wanted an ounce of hemp," (to hang himself) "he'd skip the Protestant shops, and run to Mallow-lane to buy it." Of Mallow-lane he says:—"This suburb, by its various acts of cozenage, its happy situation and possession of the weigh-houses, has branched itself into such business as almost overtops its mother. This, surely, should awaken the jealousy of all, to find the root impaired and the city impoverished, to the enriching of a set of upstart beggars" "Pray," he asks, pathetically, "is it not a very uncomfortable sight for any Protestant shopkeeper of this city to behold thatch and a skylight edificed into cant windows and slate, wherein a flat-footed Milesian shall have the impudence to have his table graced with a chaplain and pinched diaper, and in a pair of Protestant scales shall outweigh the city, and raise himself from thongs and lank hair to pumps and a periwig?" Of course, he adds, that all this is done dishonestly; "for," he continues, "when honesty was sick in Glenflesk, she crawled to Mallow-lane to die, and gave her last groan amongst the butter-buyers."

In 1773, the Penal Laws were formally relaxed. Cork made still of further advances. Protestants and Catholics entered frankly into the honourable competitions of trade. A friendly feeling and social intercourse arose between them.The "Life of Father O'Leary" (so ably written by a biographer as genial, largeminded, and eloquent as himself) affords curious instances of this intercourse. Artistic and literary tastes followed. Barry first enrolled a Corkman's name on the roll of great artists; and Berkeley, from his modest mansion in Dean-street, addressed the thinkers of every age and every land.

Cork shared the brief sunshine of Parliamentary independence. Her trade advanced with rapid strides. Her volunteer corps was the first in the South. Her citizens hailed Lord Charlemont with great enthusiasm, as they beheld his review in the Mardyke-field. In 1797, the Mayor of Cork got a collar of S.S. from the Common Speaker of the House. Civic improvements went on rapidly. The rivers through Patrick-street, Grand Parade, South Mall, and Duncan-street, were arched over, and spacious thoroughfares thus created. Patrick-street was connected with what was then called the Strand-road by Patrick's Bridge. This last improvement, indeed, was not effected without difficulty—a great meeting of citizens, held at the Council chamber, in 1785, having declared that such a bridge would be the ruin of the city.

Clouds closed again over our civic fortunes. Passions were aroused. Trade was paralysed. The Sheares plotted in their bank parlour in Patrick-street, and their ivy-trellised villa at Glasheen. Lord Edward Fitzgerald hastened to and from his hiding-place at Sunday's Well. Poor Emmet tried to combine love and war at Glanmire. Licentious German troopers once more swaggered through Cork. Peasants were again flogged, half-naked, through the streets. On the mouldering, walls of old south-gate Prison another ghastly row of bleeding skulls were seen. Thus darkly closed the last, and opened the present, century on the City of Cork.

V.—THE PERIOD OF REVIVAL.
(1803 to 1869)

One of our wisest and kindliest citizens, Dr. O'Connor, has remarked that, in some respects, the contrast between past and modern times affords a healthful correction to the tendency to "perpetual grumble" which threatens to drive all cheerfulness from the land. Religious freedom appears to me to be one of those respects. You remember how Cork-folk battled for that freedom, so long ago as the time of James the First. Ever since it has been dear to our best citizens. In this century it made large and rapid conquests. The nearly-forgotten names of Gerard Callaghan and Hely Hutchinson were at one time its watchwords. As time went on, Herbert Baldwin, William Crawford, Joseph Hayes, William Fagan, Richard Dowden,Thomas and Francis Lyons, did their share in what all now admit to have been a good work. Catholic emancipation and municipal reform were finally achieved. What more is needed, is not for us here to discuss.

For the first years of the century, trade languished. Cloth-weaving, wool-combing, glass-blowing, calico manufacture, which were carried on extensively in Cork before the

Union, were annihilated. But during the wars of Napoleon commerce revived. The trade in provisions reached vast proportions. The great Cork house of Callaghan had few rivals in the empire. The butter trade steadily increased, until its products are counted by millions. "The Customs of the Port of Cork," as Macaulay points out, "exceed the whole revenue which the whole kingdom of Ireland, in the most prosperous times, yielded to the Stuarts." Material improvements have followed. Splendid suburbs have arisen. Fine buildings have been erected. And the Harbour Board, under the guidance of Sir John Benson, have given us six miles of quayage, and brought vessels of vast tonnage to our very doors.

Amongst the earliest evidence of intellectual revival in Cork was *Bolster's Magazine*. It was published in the early years of this century, by the respected citizen whose name it bore. It had quite a brilliant staff of writers. In it appeared the earliest of Crofton Croker's legends; Dr. Maginn prac- tised the pen (which afterwards became so famous,) of "Sir Morgan O'Doherty" Millikin tried his first ballads; O'Meagher, of the *Times*, commenced to write; and the Rev. Thomas St. Laurance, the late Very Rev. Michael O'Sullivan, and the present venerable Archdeacon O'Shea, exhibited those intellectual powers which in other spheres have honoured and elevated the city. Frank MacCarthy, Joseph O'Leary, and Redmond O'Driscoll, were facile and able writers in their day. Richard Sainthill, John Windele, and James Roche, were scholars of real worth. Sheridan Knowles, Samuel Hall, and Francis Mahony, won high names in a larger arena. In our own time, several Corkmen have achieved first-class positions on the London Press, another sits on the bench at Westminster. One of our city members writes books of world-wide reputation, and mani- fests those rarer powers that enable a man "th' applause of listening senates to command". There is also a considerable diffusion of literary taste amongst the middle class in Cork. I have good reason to remember a humble home over a shop in the South Main-street, where the languages and literatures of France and Italy were household tongues and topics. Sir Walter Scott was struck with what he called " the bookishness" of Cork people. Carlyle noted the same. Thackeray, when he lodged at Grattan's-hill, remarked that, as the mercantile and professional men walked to their houses in the evening, they nearly always carried books under their arms. In art Cork has been not less distinguished. Casts of the great Greek statues, made by Canova, were presented to George IV by Pius VII and by him to the Cork Institution. These and other causes inspired quite a cluster of notable artists—Forde, Fisher, Lyster, Sheil, Brennan, Hogan, and Maclise.

But there has been a happier revival than any I have yet mentioned: that of mutual good will amongst Cork citizens of various classes, ranks, and parties. No doubt sometimes we lose temper. Some people still like to growl at each other. Others are wanting in consideration for the feelings of their neighbours. "Sweetness and light" do not always distinguish our public utterances. But, on the whole, we are steadily advancing in common sense and good will. Even those who sometimes say hot words are gentle and good-natured in the main. Differing reluctantly when we must differ; eagerly agreeing in the thousand things in which we can agree; knowing each other daily better, and liking each other the more we know, we hold out to each other in business, in society, and in life, the honest hands of friends, brothers, and fellow Cork men.

CONCLUDING OBSERVATIONS.
Thirteen centuries have now passed in review before us. Celts, Danes, Saxons, Normans, Cromwellians, Williamites; the monks of old; the rovers of the sea; the knights of

Normandy; Warbeck, and Raleigh, and Spencer; sweet "Ladye Ellen" and stout "Tom Sarsfield" haughty Don Juan, and wily Captain Muschamp, and proud Prince Rupert; Oliver Cromwell, and James II; Mac Carthy, and Sarsfield; the sufferers of the cruel penal time; Charlemont and his volunteers; Sheares, Fitzgerald, and Emmet; the politicians, artists, and literateurs of latter days; all have played their parts. We now are filling our humble places on the same little stage. Is there anything that the experience of the past suggests for the guidance of the present?

I think there is.

From all those ages past, from all those spectral lips, I hear the same solemn warning: PEACE!

To the Protestants of Cork the Ages seem to say: Give up, once for all, any idea of ascendancy over your fellow citizens. It was a mean and selfish idea at best. It has been tried often enough. It has failed. It deserved to fail.

To the Catholics of Cork the Ages seem to me to say: Give up, once for all, any idea of ascendancy over your Protestant fellow-citizens. That, too, was mean and selfish. That, too, was tried and failed. That, too, deserved to fail.

To Protestants and Catholics alike they say: with Arthur O'Leary: "Why should Religion—the sacred name of Religion—which even in an enemy discovers a brother, be any longer a wall of separation between you?" And with Berkeley: "Do you not inhabit the same spot of ground, breathe the same air, and live under the same government? Why, then, should you not conspire in one and the same design to promote the common good of your country?"

To all, the Voices of the Ages say: Sons of Celt, Dane, Saxon, and Norman! You are all Irishmen. You are all Cork men. In most of you the blood of these the noblest races of the world—are combined. Cease for ever the silly strife of race. Compromise no tittle of principle, but remember that the highest principle of all is Charity. Strike out boldly in commerce, in the professions, in literature, in art, in civic government and national affairs, for the honour and welfare of your old city. If a Cork man succeed, let every Cork man rejoice. If a Cork man fail, let every Cork man wish to lend him a hand. Be it your only rivalry who best shall serve your native land; who shall exercise the firmest self-control, the soundest sense, and the largest forbearance; who most truly in thought, and word, and deed, shall obey the primal precept of "loving one another".

From Economic Decline to the Burning of Cork

History, like beauty, is very much in the eye of the beholder. W. G. Mac Carthy, deemed it unnecessary, when addressing his mainly middle-class audience in the Cork Scientific and Literary Society, to mention the traumas the city had undergone following the Great Famine.

Slums sprouted like malignancies in the Marsh and Main Street areas, which had been recently vacated by a Catholic middle class who, with a penchant for affectation, established new suburbs with silly sounding foreign placenames like Montenotte and Tivoli (a practice echoed today on the estates of Rochestown, Douglas and *Grange,* only with snobby English-sounding estate-names instead of Italian ones).

In the ten years following the famine the city's population rose by 6%. Destitute peasants streamed into the city, cramming themselves into already densely occupied laneways and streets at a time when the population of the county overall fell by tens of thousands. Between 1851 and 1891 the county's population fell by over 200,000 — a figure higher than the city's current official population.

This depletion of people contributed to the region's industrial decline. Demand for certain local goods fell dramatically, simply because there were significantly less people about to consume them.

The coming of the railways made it easier and cheaper to import lower priced products from abroad. The only city industries that survived this traumatic period were concerns which processed agricultural products. Distilleries and breweries flourished but not without setbacks.

Ironically, Cork industries suffered from strict adherence to Quality. Merchants of the world-famous Cork Butter Exchange lost their dominance of the world butter market by failing to appreciate the growing demand among the industrialised urban poor for cheap, diluted butter products. Their quality butter proved to be just too expensive and they contemptuously refused to get involved with the new products. Likewise Irish distillers refused to exploit the world demand for light blended whiskies as produced by the Scots. The Irish believed that the supremacy of their quality product would win out in the end. They were wrong.

In spite of all this decline, or maybe even because of it, the city optimistically held a major industrial exhibition in 1883 where Fitzgerald's Park now stands. The only reminder today of that major effort of pomp is the Lord Mayor's Pavillion at the entrance to the Park, but in its day it attracted international coverage and the Prince and Princess of Wales to the city. The establishment of the electric tramways in 1898 was another boost for city confidence.

The city corporation was gradually moved to produce public housing for the poor beginning with Madden's Buildings in Blackpool. But the last city slum was cleared only as late as 1968 when the occupants of Hannover Place (where the new dole office now stands) were rehoused in the various corporation estates of Togher, Ballyphehane and Pouladuff.

Public transport in the shape of the railways and electric trams helped to extend the city boundaries in all directions, particularly towards Glanmire, Blackrock and Douglas. And eventually, many outlying villages such as Togher were absorbed in much the same way that Douglas and Ballincollig are being absorbed today.

While W. G. Mac Carthy was exhorting the Protestant and Catholic citizens of Cork to forget their differences and live together as peaceable subjects of her Brittanic Majesty a growing minority of Fenians had other ideas. The Fenians like all effective revolutionaries latched themselves onto the more popular movements such as the land agitators and Gaelic revivalists. The 1880s was a period of great rural instability with impoverished families being evicted in their thousands and the agitators committing vicious reprisals on extortionist Landlords and their agents. Eventually a leader was to emerge who inspired all of the Nationalist movements (even to a little extent the secret Irish Republican Brotherhood) to work in concert, in a pragmatic, moral, peaceable way. That man was Charles Stewart Parnell elected MP for Cork in 1880. Coinciding with his leadership of the Nationalist Party organisations such as the GAA and the Gaelic League attracted a large popular membership. A heightened perception of cultural distinction from Britain gradually developed among the urban, English-speaking populace. Under the leadership of Parnell the Nationalist Party made slow, significant gains towards the achievement of Home Rule for Ireland. But Parnell's political career was cut short by the famous Kitty O'Shea crises and the Nationalist movement started to fragment again.

When it looked as if Home Rule would at last be achieved the Unionists in North East Ulster formed a militia called the Ulster Volunteers. Armed with German guns they would fight anyone, including the British army if necessary, who might try to coerce them into a democratic self-governed Ireland dominated by the Catholic majority.

Nationalists in the South formed the Irish Volunteers as a response. But they were never as well equipped or as well organised as their Unionist opponents and were easily infiltrated by the IRB.

Arthur Griffith founded Sinn Fein as a bourgeois monarchist party whose primary aim was to establish a relationship between Ireland and Britain which was analogous to that between Hungary and Austria. Griffith envisaged a constitutional model which would have allowed an Irish parliament more independence than mere Home Rule but which would still have preserved the British Monarch as head of state. Sinn Fein was a kind of half-way house between the Nationalist Party and the Fenians who wanted nothing less than a republic. But Griffith's Sinn Fein changed radically with an influx of new young members such as Padraig Pearse who wanted a to establish a radical, independent and self-sufficient Gaelic state.

It remained a fringe movement until after the 1916 rising when the British authorities brutally executed many of the leaders. James Connolly was shot strapped to a chair because he was too weak to stand from bullet wounds. And although Connolly and most of the other participants were not members of Sinn Fein they were labelled as such by the Government and Press. *The Cork Examiner* labelled the Rising "a communistic disturbance rather than a revolutionary movement". At first the rising inspired revulsion among the Nationalist community many of whom had sons and brothers in British uniform fighting in France for the rights of little Belgium. Other Nationalists recognized the Rising as a foolhardy effort doomed to military failure from the beginning. But by May 1st *The Cork Examiner* was calling for amnesty for the insurgents. After the executions the leaders became National martyrs compared to the likes of

Wolf Tone and Robert Emmet. When the British government tried to introduce forced conscription they pushed most of the population in the direction of Sinn Fein. Frank O'Connor wrote: *It all began innocently enough. People took to attending Gaelic League concerts at which performers sang...and armed police broke them up.*

In the general election of 1918 the old Nationalist Party was virtually wiped out with Sinn Fein capturing 73 seats to the Nationalists' 6 and Unionists' 26. In Cork an electorate of 45,000 cast over 40,000 votes for the two Sinn Fein candidates James Joseph Walsh and Liam de Róiste. It was now undeniable that Sinn Fein represented the majority of Nationalist opinion. The Sinn Fein MPs resolved to abstain from Westminster and instead form an Irish parliament with its own government and ministries in Dublin.

It was not the policy of the Dail to advocate armed resistance against the British, but pockets of IRA men around the country started to raid isolated police barracks for arms and shoot-up their mainly Irish personnel. These attacks on the Royal Irish Constabulary led to vicious reprisals against the general populace with destruction of life and property. And the whole situation escalated into full-blown guerrilla warfare. The Crown forces made 20,000 raids on Irish homes between January 1919 and March 1920. Reports of these state-backed offences created a backlash against the government not only among heretofore neutral and non-committed Irishmen but in English public opinion. The IRA received a flood of new members, many of them young men who would have emigrated were it not for the intervention of the Great War and a general Government ban on emigration. Recognizing the potential of these disaffected youth the IRA, with the threat of the gun, imposed their own ban on emigration after the British government lifted theirs.

Two murders in March 1920 were a foreboding of even worse atrocities. In Dublin a septuagenarian resident magistrate Alan Bell was hauled off a tram by Republican gunmen and shot in the street in full view of everyone. No one dared to intervene. In Cork the Lord Mayor Tomás MacCurtain was shot dead at home in Blackpool, in front of his wife at 1.30 in the morning by a party of armed men with blackened faces. As MacCurtain's five children and wife mourned his brutal slaying a second party consisting of armed uniformed policemen arrived and started to tear the house apart in a search for arms. Callously stepping around the fresh corpse as they went about their business.

Tomás MacCurtain had been elected Lord Mayor the previous January when Sinn Fein won control of the city council in the Municipal and Urban elections. Terence MacSwiney was elected his deputy at the same time. Tomás MacCurtain as well as being Lord Mayor was also Commandant of the Mid-Cork Brigade of the IRA. In this connection he received many death threats, but his responsibilities as Lord Mayor prevented him from going on the run and sealed his fate. The fact that the assassins couldn't have picked a more considerate place and time to do their business was an indication of just how dirty the campaign would become.

The official police story was that MacCurtain had been killed by his own side for being too lazy an IRA commandant. Few people believed this. Before the funeral a coroner's jury found that MacCurtain *was wilfully murdered under circumstances of most callous brutality, that the murder was organised and carried out by the Royal Irish Constabulary, officially directed by the British Government.* The Jury in their rage and indignation also returned a verdict of wilful murder against Lloyd George, Lord French and Ian MacPherson as well as against three named RIC officers and others unknown of the same force. A certain D. I.

Swanzy was one of the named officers and Michael Collins had him tracked down in Lisburn and shot, Catholic premises in that town were burnt in reprisal.

The British Government refused to acknowledge publicly that a war was being waged and instead of committing the army to the conflict decided instead to provide paramilitary reinforcements to the police force in the shape of young unemployed ex-soldiers. These special recruits received only six weeks training in police duties before being unleashed on the country. Not enough constabulary uniforms were available so the men wore a miss-match of army khaki and RIC dark bottle green —as a consequence some wit christened them the *Black and Tans*.

After Tomás MacCurtain was shot his deputy Terence MacSwiney was made Mayor. He was already Commandant of the first Cork Brigade of the IRA, so it was inevitable that on August 20th 1920 the Crown Forces came to arrest him. He was charged in the middle of a city council meeting for being in possession of a police cipher and two documents *likely to cause disaffection to His Majesty.*

In protest at the continuing arrest of democratically elected public representatives MacSwiney went on hunger strike. Ten men arrested at the same time made the same decision. But while the ten men were kept in Cork prison, MacSwiney was transported via battleship to Brixton Gaol.

His hunger strike attracted world-wide attention. 300,000 Brazilian Catholics petitioned the pope to intervene on his behalf. British newspapers and even disaffected King George V pleaded publicly with the government to release him. But Lloyd George refused point blank, realising if he gave into one hunger striker he would have to give in to them all. MacSwiney's own death was preceded by that of Michael Fitzgerald, one of the Cork Prison ten. A few hours after MacSwiney a second of the Cork ten died. The rest gave up the strike at the request of Arthur Griffith.

On October 25th the seventy-fourth day of his hunger strike MacSwiney succumbed. Originally the body was to have been shipped via Hollyhead to Dublin and be at the head of a triumphant march through the length of the country to Cork. But British General Macready objected on the basis that such a move would inevitably lead to more bloodshed and disorder. So the body was sent straight to Cork. The day of the funeral October 29th was declared a day of national mourning by the Dail. A shopkeeper in Borris Co. Offaly who stayed open was boycotted and later shot. Frank O'Connor wrote in his *An Only Child*: *MacSwiney's Death on hungerstrike was watched by the whole world and cost the British Government more than a major military defeat.* MacSwiney himself had written in prison: *Facing our enemy we must declare an attitude simply. We see in their regime a thing of evil incarnate. With it there can be no parley—any more than there can be a truce with the powers of Hell. This is our simple resolution—we ask for no mercy and we will make no compromise.*

Less than two months after Lord Mayor MacSwiney's death Cork tasted destruction at the hands of the Black & Tans. On December 11th 1920, in the early evening, an IRA ambush party attacked an Auxiliary Patrol at Dillon's Cross, just up the road from the main military barracks. One officer was killed and eleven wounded. As news of the ambush spread through the streets of Cork the citizens were gripped by panic. At nine o'clock the Auxiliaries stopped the trams and ordered everyone off to be searched for guns. One priest who refused to say 'to hell with the pope' was beaten-up. By curfew the streets were deserted. At ten o'clock two houses at Dillon's Cross were set alight and firemen were prevented from putting out the flames. At about the same time the streets were filled with Auxiliaries and Black & Tans who went about shooting-off their firearms while they got drunk on beer and spirits.

Soon the sky over the city was red from the blazes in Patrick Street. Firemen had their hoses slashed by the Black & Tans and were prevented from switching on fire hydrants. Auxiliaries, Black & Tans and British soldiers, looted the shops they burnt. A second group less interested in looting burnt down the city hall and city library. Some women of the city joined in on the looting and were seen dancing in the street with the drunken military. Farcically as some Black & Tans set more fires other Black & Tans with the help of regular soldiers tried to put them out.

The whole north side of Cork viewed the spectacle from their windows and gardens. The next day Patrick Street could be viewed as a wasteland. Twenty-one Patrick Street shops had been completely destroyed. Altogether forty-four shops were burnt to the ground, twenty-four partially damaged and many more looted. Miraculously nobody in the city was killed. The total damage was estimated to be £3,000,000. Frank O'Connor wrote: *Later I Stood at the corner of Dillon's Cross where the ambush had been and saw a whole block of little houses demolished by a British tank.* Sean O'Faolain wrote: *It all made a blaze as comparatively wicked, destructive and terrifying as a bad blitz attack on central London.* Richard Bennet in his book the Black & Tans wrote: *Over Thirty years later an old and unrepentant Black and Tan, by that time dressed in the respected uniform of a Chelsea Pensioner, was asked to account for the behaviour of the Crown Forces on that night. 'Well you see,' he said after a moment's reflection, 'it was near Christmas.'*

Calls for an independent inquiry came from both Sinn Fein and Unionist groups who were equally aghast at the police's disrespect for the sanctity of private property.

In Westminster, Cabinet Minister Sir Hamer Greenwood denied that the fires were started by the police or army and suggested that it was the people of Cork themselves who had started the fire. He further suggested that the Library and City Hall were not set ablaze deliberately but that the flames had spread from Patrick Street. Evidently nobody briefed him that the untouched South Mall and the Lee were between the two sites of destruction. Greenwood lost all credibility for himself and his government with this speech. Soon afterwards a British Labour Party Commission sent to the city to investigate the burning were held-up by Auxiliaries and threatened with shooting.

The war did not last long afterwards, the propaganda defeats resulting from the deaths of Cork's two Lord Mayors and the destruction of her centre contributed to the pressure on Lloyd George to agree to meet a Sinn Fein delegation and propose a treaty.

Following a long saga of ethnic and religious strife Cork, since independence, has been a city noted for the tolerance of its citizens, a city where people of different race, nationality, creed and sexual orientation live in peace and mutual respect. However the economic struggle, the struggle to provide wealth and meaningful occupations for all her citizens, continues.

— Pat Cotter

Bibliography/further reading
Sean Beecher: *The Story of Cork.* Mercier 1971
Sean Beecher: *Cork Day by Day* Collins Press 1993
Andy Bielenberg: *Cork's Industrial Revolution 1780-1800: Development or Decline?* Cork University Press 1991
Richard Bennett: *The Black and Tans* London 1959
Frank O'Connor: *An Only Child* Macmillan & Co. 1961
Sean O'Faolain: *Vive Moi* Sinclair-Stevenson 1993
Michael Martin *History of Cork* articles 40 & 41 Cork Examiner 1985
P. O'Flanagan *Cork: History and Society* Geography publications 1993